Legends of Rock & Roll

Bobby Darin

An unauthorized fan tribute

By: James Hoag

Paperback Edition

Manufactured in the United States of America

Other Paperbacks

by

James Hoag

Legends of Rock and Roll Series

Legends of Rock & Roll Volume 1 - The Fifties

Legends of Rock & Roll Volume 2 - The Sixties

Legends of Rock & Roll Volume 3 - The Seventies

The Beatles, Queen

Individual Beatles

John Lennon, Paul McCartney, George Harrison,

Ringo Starr

Fifties

Everly Brothers, Little Richard, Fats Domino,

Jerry Lee Lewis, Paul Anka, Rick Nelson,

Connie Francis

Sixties

Neil Diamond, Roy Orbison, The Beach Boys,

Bob Dylan, The Doors, The Bee Gees,

The Grateful Dead, Simon & Garfunkel, The Monkees

The Four Seasons

Seventies

Eagles, Bruce Springsteen

Eighties

Madonna

Legends of Country Music

Reba McEntire, Willie Nelson, Johnny Cash,

George Jones, Merle Haggard, Garth Brooks,

Waylon Jennings

(All Available at Amazon.com)

Table of Contents

INTRODUCTION

Almost everyone remembers where they were when they heard that President Kennedy was shot (if you're old enough). I remember where I was when I heard that Elvis Presley died. I also remember where I was when I heard that Bobby Darin had died. We all knew it was a possibility. He had been having problems for several years and we, his public, hoped he would lick this and come back stronger than before. But, it was not to be and Bobby Darin died after having open heart surgery on December 20, 1973, just before Christmas. It was a sad Christmas for his family and all his fans.

I remember thinking that if I could be any entertainer performing in the U.S. in the late Fifties and early Sixties; Bobby Darin would be in my Top 5. Everyone wanted to be Elvis and there were other guys who always had the girls, but Bobby Darin married Sandra Dee ("Look at me, I'm Sandra Dee."). What could be better than that?

There's been considerable discussion about whether Bobby Darin should be classified as a rock & roll singer, a Vegas hipster cat, an interpreter of popular standards, or even a folk-rocker. He was all of these and none of these. He was a complicated man who knew he didn't have long on this earth and made the best of the time he had.

As with the other "Legend of Rock & Roll" books, this is not an exhaustive biography. There are others which cover his life much more thoroughly. "Dream Lovers" by Dodd Daren is one of these. I am mostly interested in the music, the effect it had on me and on America. I cover his life so as to put the music into perspective.

HIS YOUTH

Bobby Darin was born Walden Robert Cassotto on May 14, 1936 at the height of the Great Depression. His early life sounds like it comes straight from a soap opera. He was born in the Bronx, New York City to a working class family. His family was of Italian descent. The man who Bobby thought was his father, Saverio Antonio Cassotto, was actually his grandfather and Saverio died just a few months before Bobby was born. Bobby never knew his father.

Like so many people who end up extremely successful, Bobby started out poor. Bobby once said that the crib that he slept in was really just a cardboard box. No one knows if this is true. He was raised by his mother, Vivian Fern (Walden) Cassotto who everyone called Polly. He had an older sister named Giovannina Juliette Cassotto who also helped raise him. They called her Nina. Since Nina was older, she eventually married and moved out of the house.

In 1968, when Bobby was 32 years old, Nina came to him while he was playing in New Jersey and confessed that she was, in fact, his mother. The woman, Polly, who he thought was his mother was his grandmother and the man he thought was his father, was his grandfather. Like I said, a real soap opera.

It was Polly who would take little Bobby into New York to see what was left of vaudeville. This was the early Forties, the war was on and vaudeville had pretty much died. But Bobby was able to see people like Sophie Tucker and this was what first got him interested in a music career.

Bobby was frail and sickly as a child. Starting at about age eight, he had several bouts of rheumatic fever. Rheumatic fever is a disease which attacks the heart valves and so Bobby lived with a weak heart the rest of his life. A doctor mentioned to Polly that he would be lucky if he saw sixteen. Of course, we all know that Bobby beat the odds even though it was his heart that finally killed him.

A TALENT FOR MUSIC

He did have an innate talent for music. By the time he was in his teens, he could play the piano, drums and guitar. He later learned other instruments and, of course, he learned to sing. As a boy, his best friend was singer Dick Roman. You may not have heard of Roman, but he too, like Bobby, aspired to be a singer and did cut a couple albums. He never caught on and lived his short life trying to make it to the top. He died of a heart attack at the age of 38. While Bobby was two years older than Roman, they lived just about the same number of years, best friends in youth, one making it big, one not so much and both dying of heart problems.

Bobby Cassotto was an outstanding student as a youth. He graduated from the Bronx High School of Science and received a scholarship to attend Hunter College of the City University of New York as a theater major. Bobby was tired of going to school, though, and wanted to start performing, so after only one year, he dropped out of Hunter and started playing nightclubs in and around New York City. He even played the resorts in the Catskill Mountains in upstate New York.

It was sometime during this early period that Bobby changed his professional name to Darin. It is rumored that Bobby saw a Chinese neon sign over a restaurant that advertised [Man]Darin Duck (with the bulbs that spelled MAN burned out) and that was where he got the name. Others say he just picked it out of a phone book. I like the Chinese sign version better. There is no proof of any of this, however.

Unlike some of the others I have spotlighted in the Legends of Rock & Roll series, Bobby didn't have his parents to push him or to help him with connections. Bobby was entirely self-motivated, He created his own band for which he sang and played the drums. He started songwriting. He was friends with another Bronx High School Alumni,

Don Kirshner. Kirshner was one of the original, great music producers. He was responsible for the careers of many singers and performers of the Fifties and Sixties. People like Neil Diamond, Carole King and The Monkees. Kirshner was to become instrumental in getting Bobby's career off the ground.

In 1956, Bobby's manager signed him to a contract with Decca Records. It seemed like a good move, Bill Haley and the Comets recorded for Decca as did a lot of other big names of the time.

SONG WRITER

You may have heard of the Brill Building. It is a building in New York located at 1619 Broadway on 49th Street just north of Times Square. This is where young aspiring song writers would assemble and, well, write songs. That is where Carole King started as well as Neil Sedaka, Paul Simon, Neil Diamond and many, many more. The building has been described as "the most important generator of popular songs in the Western world."

Bobby Darin became one of the pack of song writers that frequented the Brill Building. It was while he was there that he was introduced to Connie Francis. She was just starting out and needed material to record. Francis was not a song writer and turned to Bobby for help. The two became very close and actually talked about eloping and getting married. Connie's father found out about the plan and chased Bobby away with a pistol. He told Bobby to never see his daughter again. Connie's father told her Bobby was a "bum, he ain't goin' nowhere." Bobby only saw Connie Francis two more times in his life and by then he was married himself. Connie remarked that not marrying Bobby Darin was the biggest mistake of her life.

Bobby and Connie liked to have dates at the "Apollo Theater" in Harlem, New York City. They boasted that they were the only two white people in the theater. Bobby was affected by the black music of the Fifties and for his first record for Decca, he recorded "Rock Island Line" which was an old Leadbelly number. However, to make it more palatable for the white audience, he did the Lonnie Donegan's skiffle version which was much more "white" sounding. Donegan had a number 8 hit on the Billboard charts in 1956 with "Rock Island Line", but he is much better known for the silly "Does Your Chewing Gum Lose It's Flavor (On the Bedpost Over Night)" which peaked at number 5 in 1961.

Bobby sang "Rock Island Line" on a CBS program called "Stage Show". This was his television debut. He was so nervous, he wrote the words to the song on his palms in case he forgot them. He did. Even with the TV exposure, his songs really didn't do too much. After recording four records with Decca (and no album), nothing was happening. His records had not charted and so Bobby decided to change labels and maybe change his luck. Leaving Decca, he signed with Atlantic Records (Atco) and started fresh. He still wrote songs for others, but now he started writing songs for himself.

His first record with Atco was "I Found a Million Dollar Baby" written by Harry Warren. It was 1957 and Elvis Presley was the biggest thing on radio and television, so Bobby decided to do the song in Elvis's style and do a rocking version of the song. But, Bobby Darin was not really a teen idol. He looked older than his years. He worried about his appearance. He was losing his hair and he told his manager, Steve Blauner, that when he looked into a mirror, he saw "an ugly, small Italian man".

SPLISH SPLASH

But Bobby's problem wasn't his appearance; he just needed the right song. In 1958, he wrote (with famous DJ Murray "The K" Kaufman") and sang his break out hit "Splish Splash". The song originated from a bet Kaufman had made with his mother. She bet him he couldn't write a song which started "Splish splash, I was taking a bath" and to win the bet, he and Bobby did. Bobby later said he wrote it in 12 minutes. It is this song, more than any other which proves that Bobby Darin deserves to be called "rock and roll". The song was an instant hit, peaking at number 3 on the Hot 100, selling over a million copies. I remember it well. I loved songs that mentioned other songs in the words. In "Splish Splash", there's a party going on and Lollipop is there and Peggy Sue and, of course, Good Golly Miss Molly, all great songs from 1957 and 58.

The next song Bobby wrote was called "Early in the Morning". For some reason, since he was still under contract to Atlantic, he took it to Brunswick records and recorded it under the name "The Ding Dongs". As you might expect, Atlantic found out about it. I'm surprised they did not fire Bobby right on the spot. Brunswick was forced to turn over the masters to Atlantic and that would have been the end of it, except that the song was getting airplay in the New York area. So, Atlantic (Atco) released the record with the artist name of "The Rinky Dinks". The song reached number 24 on the US charts. Now, you might remember the song being done by Buddy Holly and the Crickets. They are better known for the song, but they only reached number 32 in the U.S.. In the U.K., the song was released under Bobby Darin's own name. So we have the unusual occurrence of one song being released having three different artist names, but all being the exact same song. I suspect the Brunswick version is valuable today, I wish I had a copy of it.

Bobby's next song was "Queen of the Hop" which was another in the same style as "Splish Splash". Bobby was still rockin'. He wrote "Queen of the Hop" and mentioned some of the same girls he had in "Splish Splash". "Well, you can talk about your Julie (a song by the Crescendos) and your Peggy Sue (done by Buddy Holly). You can keep your Miss Molly (from Little Richard's Good Golly Miss Molly) and your Mary Lou (a Ricky Nelson song.)" Bobby had a formula and he was sticking to it. "Queen" rose to number 9 on the Hot 100 and became his second million seller.

Next, in 1959, was a song which I don't remember at all. It's called "Plain Jane". You can find it on YouTube and it was based on the old traditional standard "Buffalo Gals". Instead of "Buffalo Gals, won't you come out tonight," the words are "Plain Jane, won't you come out tonight." It's a fairly silly song, but still enjoyable to listen to.

Bobby's third million seller was "Dream Lover" and it signaled, I believe, a subtle change in Bobby Darin's music. It is still an up tempo song but is not in the same mode as the novelty songs that he had been doing. "I want a dream lover so I don't have to dream alone." You might say, Bobby was maturing, growing up a little. It has been called a "soulful rock song" and I couldn't agree more. Something you may not know is that Neil Sedaka plays piano on the song. "Dream Lover" has certainly become a classic, being done by many other artists. It was Bobby's biggest hit up to that point, peaking at number two in 1959.

MACK THE KNIFE

But his biggest was yet to come. And the song which cemented Bobby Darin into the minds and hearts of all American's and, I think, people the world over was his next hit, "Mack the Knife". Now the teenage singer of novelty songs was gone and in its place, a mature, respected singer who could take his act to Vegas or anywhere else he desired.

The song originated in a 1928 German stage drama, known in English as *The Threepenny Opera*. The main character was a character named Macheath who was truly a scoundrel. The play told of Macheath's foul deeds. He was a thief, a murderer and a rapist. Not the kind of leading character that one would think could be the subject of a number one American hit record. But it was.

After an English translation of the song was made, in 1956, "The Theme from Threepenny Opera" was a pretty big hit in American being done by several artists, including Dick Hyman, Richard Hayman & Jan August and even Lawrence Welk, but these were all very slow, instrumental versions. Listening to Lawrence Welk's version, I have a hard time connecting that song with Bobby Darin's version of "Mack the Knife". Louis Armstrong jazzed it up and added words. "The Theme from Threepenny Opera" was subtitled (Mack the Knife). This is the version Bobby Darin went with in 1959.

Bobby's version of "Mack the Knife" was his first number one hit, remaining for nine weeks, and it went on to be the Billboard number one hit for the entire year of 1959. It reached number 6 on the R&B charts and it earned a Grammy as Record of the Year. Bobby was also voted Best New Artist at the Grammy's that year. And the song has subsequently been inducted into the Grammy Hall of Fame. Surprisingly, Dick Clark, of American Bandstand, told him not to record it. He said that a song with Opera in its title would not be played by the teenagers of the day. But Bobby refused "to play it safe" and that one decision changed his life. They took the words Threepenny Opera out of the title and it just became "Mack the Knife". The kids loved it and since it had an adult appeal as well, the parents loved it too.

Frank Sinatra, who recorded the song himself, later called Bobby's version "the definitive version". In 2008, Billboard put together a list of the All-Time Top 100 songs. "Mack the Knife" was number three. Unfortunately, "Mack the Knife" was Bobby Darin's only number one song. This turned out to be the peak of his career as far as Hot 100 charts were concerned. From this point on, Bobby left the world of rock & roll and became a more mainstream, crooner type singer. He very much wanted to be another Frank Sinatra. In 1959 he told Life Magazine, "I want to be a legend by 25."

Remember Dick Roman, Bobby's friend from his youth? Roman was offered "Mack the Knife" first, before Bobby. But he turned it down. Would it have been as big a hit with Roman as voice? Nobody knows, but I'll bet Roman never forgave himself.

BEYOND THE SEA

Besides "Mack the Knife", the song that Bobby is probably most known for is "Beyond the Sea". Bobby was no longer writing his own songs. "Beyond the Sea" is based on a French song by Charles Trenet called "La Mer" which, of course, means "The Sea". The song was a standard of sorts, having been recorded by Benny Goodman in the Forties and again by Mantovani and Roger Williams in the Fifties. Bobby's version, however, is probably the best known.

Because of his new direction in music choice, Bobby was now popular at famous nightclubs in New York and Las Vegas. In Las Vegas, he appeared with George Burns at the Sahara Club and the two became lifelong friends. He appeared many times at the Copacabana in New York, which had to add seating whenever Bobby was there to accommodate the crowds of people that wanted to see him. Walter Winchell wrote on June 7, 1960: "Darin, 24, opened a sensational engagement at the famed nightclub last Thursday night and has been playing to capacity throngs since. It was his first New York engagement after making show-business history on the West Coast."

He also played often at the Sands Hotel in Las Vegas. This was the famous hotel where the "Rat Pack" played, Frank Sinatra, Dean Martin, Sammy Davis Jr., Joey Bishop and Peter Lawford. Because of "Mack the Knife", Bobby fit right in with the crowd that loved the Rat Pack guys. It is said that Sammy Davis Jr. remarked that Bobby Darin was "the only person I never wanted to follow".

He was featured on the television show "This is Your Life" in 1959 which included George Burns and several relatives and friends. Bobby was very good at discovering new talent. He found Richard Prior, Wayne Newton and Flip Wilson, all struggling performers at this time. Bobby would have them open for him and we all know what happened to them. They all became giant stars in their own right. In an era when whites and blacks did not mix, Bobby insisted that black comedian, George Kirby open for him at the Copacabana. Because Bobby was so big, they allowed it.

Bobby also owned a record company in the Sixties called TM Music/Trio. Working with new artists was a passion of Bobby's and since he let Wayne Newton open for him in Vegas, he also signed Newton to TM. He gave him a song that was originally written for Bobby, "Danke Schoen". As you probably know, Wayne Newton took that song to number 13 in 1963. But don't let the fact that it didn't reach number one let you think that this wasn't a big deal. "Danke Schoen" became Wayne Newton's signature song. And Wayne Newton eventually became "Mr. Las Vegas". He still plays there today and it is my understanding that "Danke Schoen" is sung at every concert. All thanks to Bobby Darin.

Another student of Bobby Darin was Roger McGuinn who played guitar and sang backup vocals on Bobby's records and also played in his band when they were on the road. You may not know the name Roger McGuinn, but I'll bet you've heard of the Byrds. The Byrds were a great band who charted from 1965 until 1967. They had two number one hits during that time, "Mr. Tambourine Man" and "Turn, Turn, Turn". When I was listening to music in the Sixties, I assumed that the Byrds were British and part of the British Invasion. They had a sound like bands from England that were charting at the time. But The Byrds were organized in Los Angeles and Roger McGuinn was from Chicago and he owes a lot of his future success to Bobby Darin.

THE DECLINE

In 1962, Bobby began to write more country music. This was true of a lot of the performers of that time period. Rock and roll seemed to be dying away. The early Sixties was not a time for great music. Sales were falling. The industry needed a good shot in the arm. That shot came in 1964 in the form of the Beatles. What they brought to the music scene and the dozens of other performers from across the pond was to rejuvenate the business and make us want to listen to music again. However, if you were not British, things were tough. There are exceptions, of course, but Bobby had seen his best times and was struggling.

He recorded "Things" which has a country flare in 1962 and it got to number 3 on the Hot 100 and peaked at number 2 in the U.K. He deserted Atlantic for Capitol for a few years where he recorded "You're the Reason I'm Living" (#3) in 1963. This song was covered on the Country charts, but no version did very well. Then "Eighteen Yellow Roses" (#10) also in 1963. In 1966, he came back to Atlantic where he had his last Top 10 record with "If I Were a Carpenter" which peaked at number 8. There was only one more charted hit after that and Bobby finished his chart career with "Lovin' You" (#32) in 1967. That was his last Top 40 song.

ACTING CAREER

A lot of people remember Bobby Darin as an actor just as much as they remember him as a singer. I have listed most of the movies he was in below the discography below. It's quite a list. He started with a TV show called "Dan Raven" in 1960. He played himself in two episodes. In 1960, he was the only actor ever to be signed to five major Hollywood film studios.

It appears that the first movie he actually acted in was called "Pepe", a comedy which starred Cantinflas as Pepe. It was a musical and all Bobby did was sing, but it was a start. The movie also included such stars as Bing Crosby and Sammy Davis Jr., among others. It is a really fun movie if you get a chance to catch it on late night TV, you will enjoy it.

He wrote music for several films and sang on the soundtracks of some. He performed the opening and closing songs on the soundtrack of Disney's "That Darn Cat" in 1965. His first major film role was "Come September" in 1961. The movie also starred Rock Hudson and Gina Lollobrigida. "Come September" was shot in Italy and it was in Italy that Bobby met his future wife, Sandra Dee. This movie was obviously aimed at the teenage demographic that mostly bought his records. To attract the young boys, the movie producers cast an 18 year old Sandra Dee as Bobby's love interest in the movie.

Sandra Dee remembers seeing Bobby for the first time standing on the shore when her boat was docking nearby. Bobby, never one to hesitate when he was going after something, immediately knew he liked what he saw. "Will you marry me?" He called to her. Remember, this was the first time they had met. "Not today", she answered back, knowing he was just joking. Bobby continued to ask her every day of the movie shoot and eventually he got the answer he was looking for.

Bobby Darin and Sandra Dee fell in love. They were married on December 1, 1960, after returning to the states at the completion of the movie, probably breaking thousands of young girl's hearts all over the world. The marriage lasted seven years and they broke up in 1967. They did have one son, Dodd Mitchell Darin (born 1961) who was a big part of Bobby's life, even after the divorce.

Bobby also got a role in the musical "State Fair" in 1962 which starred Pat Boone, Ann-Margret, Pamela Tiffin, Tom Ewell, and veteran actress Alice Faye (she started with Rudy Valle back in the Thirties). He played a TV reporter who becomes involved with a farm girl played by Tiffin. The movie was not a big hit, but the music was great and the soundtrack became a best seller.

Bobby wanted to be taken seriously as an actor. He tried out for more meaningful roles. He started his own production company called Sandar Productions to help his career. He wanted to do it all. He always knew he wouldn't be on this earth long and he wanted as much as he could get while he was here. He said in 1962 "Someday I want an Academy Award." He never did win an Academy Award, but he did win a Golden Globe. That was as close as he got.

He appeared in four other films during 1962. His first dramatic role was in John Cassavetes' film "Too Late Blues" which was a war drama. He did "Hell Is For Heroes" which starred Steve McQueen, James Coburn, and Fess Parker. Next was "Pressure Point" with Sidney Poitier which earned him a Golden Globe for Most Promising Male Newcomer. After that he was back with (his now wife), Sandra Dee in "If a Man Answers", another comedy in which he wrote and sang all the music. 1962 was a busy year for Bobby Darin. How many of us could have accomplished all of that in a year.

He was nominated for an Academy Award for Best Supporting Actor for the film "Captain Newman, M.D." which starred Gregory Peck, Angie Dickinson, and Larry Storch. He played a decorated WW II aviator and psychiatric patient who believes he's a coward for not saving his friend from a burning plane. At the Cannes Film Festival he won the French Film Critics Award for Best Actor for the film.

He starred again with his wife Sandra Dee in the 1965 film "*That Funny Feeling*", also writing and singing the movie's theme.

THREE PERSONAL BLOWS

In 1967, Bobby and Sandra Dee's marriage ended. She felt that Bobby was ignoring his family to pursue fame and money. He was left with his son, Dodd, who he adored, but the failure of the marriage was a major blow to Bobby.

Bobby Darin had always thought of himself as a political person, and in 1965, he participated in the march for civil rights from Selma to Montgomery, Alabama. He was an early supporter of the Rev. Dr. Martin Luther King. We already talked about the times when he would insist on using black artists as his opening acts, kick starting several careers, like Richard Pryor and Flip Wilson.

In 1968, he joined the campaign of Robert Kennedy who was on the trail looking to be nominated for President. As I mentioned in the introduction, those of us who were living at the time remember when John Kennedy was shot. I think the same goes for Robert Kennedy, although maybe not as strong. This was the third major assassination in this country during the Sixties including Martin Luther King. Bobby was working on Kennedy's campaign and was in the Ambassador Hotel in Los Angeles, California when Robert Kennedy was shot. This affected Bobby greatly. He was devastated and literally went into hiding for months afterward.

It was about this time that he found out that his mother was really his grandmother and his sister was really his mother. "My whole life has been a lie", Bobby remarked. All of this happened in a fairly short period of time and led to bouts of depression and feelings that Bobby could not deal with.

His career stagnating, he sold his home in Los Angeles and moved into a trailer at Big Sur, California. He lived there, alone, for nearly a year, not performing and not recording. He started another record label called Direction Records. This was 1969 and protests against the Vietnam War were prevalent across the country. A lot of the music being played was protest music. Bobby, being politically motivated and very much against the war, decided to use Direction records to spotlight performers who sang folk and protest oriented music. The first single he released on Direction was "Long Line Rider", a protest song. He debuted the song at the Cocoanut Grove in October of 1968. Two months later, in January, 1969, he sang it at the Copacabana in New York. When he planned to sing it on the Jackie Gleason show that spring, he was told he couldn't, the song was too controversial. So, he walked off the show.

He next wrote the song "Simple Song of Freedom" another protest song which did not chart. It was a minor hit for Tim Hardin, however.

When the Seventies began, the folk era was pretty much done. The Vietnam War was resolved and people didn't have as much to protest. Bobby ventured out to start singing his old standards again. He hadn't sang "Mack the Knife" for quite some time, being so heavily involved in the anti-Vietnam War movement. He returned the song to his repertoire. He was playing Vegas again. He also included some Creedence Clearwater songs that were "safe". He started looking for a new record label. This time he joined Motown records and recorded three albums for them. He also did a couple more films.

In January of 1971, he was rushed to the hospital for the first of several open-heart surgeries to fix the damage that had been done by the rheumatic fever in his youth. They inserted plastic heart values to replace his values which were worn out. Six months later, he returned to performing.

A COMEBACK

Starting a sort of comeback, Bobby was again playing in Vegas. On September 1, 1971, he appeared at Harrah's in Vegas. These last years he played in Vegas were the most successful he had had in a decade. They literally re-started his career. He got his own television show on NBC called "Dean Martin Presents The Bobby Darin Amusement Company". The first show was July 27, 1972 and was meant to be a summer replacement show and only lasted for six episodes. It was mostly a variety show with comedy sketches and, of course, music. Bobby sang a lot on the show. Like many of the great performers before him, Bobby liked to do characters in the sketches. He was particularly fond of Groucho Marx and he did an uncanny imitation of the great comic. There was also "The Godmother" with Bobby dressed in drag. And "Dusty John Dustin" who was a beatnik poet accompanied by bongo drums.

After the successful summer run, NBC decided to bring the show back. "The Bobby Darin Show" debuted in January of 1973, but it was really the same show. This show would run until his death. He got married for the second time in June of 1973 to Andrea Yeager who was a beautiful legal secretary but it only lasted about 4 months. He continued to be a top draw in Vegas.

In late February 1972, *New York Times* reporter Don Heckman made this observation in a review of a Bobby Darin performance at the Copacabana:

"Elusive though his style may be — folksy-humble at some points, Vegas-flashy at others –Darin is still a first-class performer. He sang, played the guitar, drums and piano, tied things together with a virtually nonstop and often with witty patter, and managed to pull a lackadaisical first-night audience out of its lethargy.

"Still, Darin belongs to another era, despite his eager efforts to keep up-to-date with songs like Tim Hardin's "If I Were a Carpenter" and his own "Sing A Simple Song of Freedom." He is clearly most comfortable with the Frank Sinatra-Dean Martin style that was the essence of his first musical incarnation. . . .""

THE END

Late in 1973, Bobby's health took a turn for the worse. The heart problems came back and it looked like he needed more surgery. He failed to take the appropriate antibiotic before he had dental work done (something that anyone with a history of rheumatic fever must do). He developed a systemic infection, otherwise known as sepsis.

This damaged one of his already faulty heart values. On December 11, 1973, he was admitted to Cedar-Sinai Medical Center in Los Angeles to repair two artificial heart values that he had received during his earlier surgery in January of 1971. On December 19, after a six hour surgery to repair the heart values, Bobby was placed in the recovery room. There, sometime after midnight on December 20, 1973, Bobby Darin died, without regaining consciousness.

There was no funeral, but the world mourned. Bobby had left instructions that his body be donated to science and it was. His remains were sent to UCLA Medical Center as per his instructions. After his death, his furniture and piano were donated to Regina Hall, a home for unmanageable girls in Las Vegas.

BOBBY DARIN, THE MAN

Not many knew it but Bobby was a true genius. He had an IQ of 137 which put him in the top 2%. He was very political (on the liberal side) and we already talked about his relationship with Robert Kennedy, Bobby was friends with a number of politicians. He considered, at one time, going into politics himself, but never acted on it. He was in show business for 22 years and, of course, that should have been much longer. He had a gift for comedy as well as music. He could do impersonations of many different people, including James Cagney, Jerry Lewis, Groucho Marx, Ray Charles, Marlon Brando and many others.

He danced. He had great gusto and enthusiasm for everything he did, in spite of his health. He played several instruments including the piano, drums and guitar. His friend and manager Jay Tell said of him: "Excellence was his goal. Self-confident outside, down deep he was sincere, unpretentious, yet seriously misunderstood. Lifelong pain affected his music, but never lessened his commitment to do his best every time."

He worked hard, perhaps too hard. It is said that he did each show as if it were his last. And eventually, it was. I believe he finally achieved the "star" status that he wanted so badly as a youth and so richly deserved as a adult. Bobby Darin was one of the best.

LEGACY OF BOBBY DARIN

Bobby Darin was inducted into the Rock and Roll Hall of Fame in 1990. Dodd Darin, his son gave the acceptance speech. Paul Anka (a probable future Legends of Rock & Roll candidate) also spoke about Bobby at the ceremony. In 1999, he was inducted into the Songwriters Hall of Fame. He also has a star on the Hollywood Walk of Fame for Recording at 1735 Vine Street in Hollywood, California. And let's not forget that in 2007, he was inducted into the Hit Parade Hall of Fame. It's too bad that he wasn't here to enjoy all of that.

In 1994, his son with Sandra Dee, Dodd wrote the biography "Dream Lovers: The magnificent shattered lives of Bobby Darin and Sandra Dee by their son Dodd Darin" The book is still available.

Remember "Rock and Roll Heaven" by The Righteous Brothers. They sing "If there's a rock and roll heaven, you know they got a hell of a band". Then after mentioning several of the great artists who had passed on at that time, they honor Bobby with "and Bobby gave us Mack the Knife, lookout he's back in town." You can hear the whole song on YouTube.

In May of 2007, Bobby was awarded a star on the Las Vegas Walk of Stars to acknowledge the contribution he made to Las Vegas over the years. They called him one the greatest entertainers of the Twentieth Century. If he had lived, he would probably still be playing there right next to Wayne Newton.

An interesting bit of trivia relates to the TV show "American Dreams" which played for a couple years back around 2003. Duncan Sheik, a singer of the time, played Bobby Darin in an episode of the show and performed "Beyond the Sea"

And then there was the movie of the same name as the song, "Beyond the Sea". Director Barry Levinson had wanted to do a biopic of Bobby Darin as early as 1986, but the project didn't get off the ground until 1997. By this time, Levinson was on to other projects and so Kevin Spacey picked up the ball and, with Bobby's son Dodd, they acquired the film rights and made the film. "Beyond the Sea" opened in 2004 at the Toronto International Film Festival. Kevin Spacey played Bobby and Kate Bosworth played Sandra Dee. Spacey made the decision to do all the singing himself and, I think, did an outstanding job. Spacey is not known for his singing ability, but "Beyond the Sea" was a great attempt.

Unfortunately, it didn't go over too well with the critics and the public really didn't flock to the theaters to see it. But it did generate new interest in Bobby Darin and so the record companies re-released several of his albums. Spacey did receive a Golden Globe nomination for best actor for the film, but lost to Jamie Foxx, who, ironically, won for his portrayal of Ray Charles in the movie "Ray". Ray Charles could be a future Legends of Rock & Roll candidate, also.

AFTERWORD

Bobby Darin was born in 1936. That means, if he had lived, he would be, as of this writing, 75 years old. He's been gone 38 years and I still miss him. In preparing this short report, I listened to most of his music from the Fifties and Sixties. It was great to go back and remember just how good a talent he was.

If you have read any of my other "tributes" to the rock and roll era, you know that I grew up in the Fifties. I graduated from high school in 1960, so the last four years of the Fifties are my era for music. I love the music of the Fifties (and the Sixties). Bobby Darin was on my list of the artists I most liked to listen to.

You can contact me at www.number1project.com where I occasionally blog about things that interest me in the music world (mostly, the twentieth century). Go find it and read it and leave me a comment. I also have a Facebook fan page called "Legends of Rock & Roll". You can comment there, too. If you love the music as much as I do, you'll enjoy the trip. Thanks for reading.

ABOUT THE AUTHOR

James Hoag has always been a big fan of Rock & Roll. Most people graduate from high school and then proceed to "grow up" and go on to more adult types of music. James got stuck at about age 18 and has been an avid fan of popular music ever since. His favorite music is from the Fifties, the origin of Rock & Roll and which was the era in which James grew up. But he likes almost all types of popular music including country music.

After working his entire life as a computer programmer, he is now retired, and he decided to share his love of the music and of the performers by writing books that discuss the life and music of the various people who have meant so much to him over the years.

He calls each book a "love letter" to the stars that have enriched our lives so much. These people are truly Legends.

SELECTED DISCOGRAPHY

Albums

1958 "Bobby Darin" Atco

1959 "That's All" Atco

1960 "This is Darin" Atco

1960 "Darin At The Copa" Atco

1960 "For Teenagers Only" Atco

1960 "It's You Or No One" Atco

1960 "The 25th Day of December" Atco

1961 "Two Of A Kind (Bobby Darin & Johnny Mercer)" Atco

1961 "The Bobby Darin Story" Atco

1961 "Love Swings" Atco

1961 "Twist with Bobby Darin" Atco

1962 "Bobby Darin Sings Ray Charles" Atco

1962 "Things and Other Things" Atco

1962 "Oh! Look at Me Now" Capitol

1963 "Earthy" Capitol

1963 "You're the Reason I'm Living" Capitol

1963 "18 Yellow Roses" Capitol

1963 "Golden Folk Hits" Capitol

1964 "Winners" Atco

1964 "As Long As I'm Singing" Capitol

1964 "From Hello Dolly to Goodbye Charlie" Capitol

1965 "Venice Blue" Capitol

1966 "The Best Of Bobby Darin" Capitol

1966 "The Shadow of Your Smile" Atlantic

1966 "In A Broadway Bag" Atlantic

1966 "If I Were a Carpenter" Atlantic

1967 "Inside Out" Atlantic

1967 "Bobby Darin Sings Doctor Dolittle" Atlantic

1968 "Bobby Darin Born Walden Robert Cassotto" Direction

1969 "Commitment" Direction

1972 "Finally" Motown

1972 "Bobby Darin" Motown

1974 "Darin: 1936-1973" Motown

Singles

1956 "Rock Island Line" Decca

1956 "Silly Willy" Decca

1956 "The Greatest Builder of Them All" Decca

1957 "Dealer In Dreams" Decca

1957 "Million Dollar Baby" Atco

1957 "Don't Call My Name" Atco

1958 "Silly Willy" Decca

1958 "Just In Case You Change Your Mind" Atco

1958 "Splish Splash" Atco

1958 "Early in the Morning" Brunswick

1958 "Queen of the Hop" Atco

1958 "Mighty Mighty Man" Atco

1959 "Plain Jane" Atco

1959 "Dream Lover" Atco

1959 "Mack the Knife" Atco

1960 "Beyond the Sea" Atco

1960 "Clementine" Atco

1960 "Won't You Come Home Bill Bailey?" Atco

1960 "Beachcomber" Atco

1960 "Artificial Flowers" Atco

1960 "Christmas Auld Lang Syne" Atco

1960 "She's Tanfastic" Atco

1961 "Lazy River" Atco

1961 "Nature Boy" Atco

1961 "Theme from 'Come September'" Atco

1961 "You Must Have Been a Beautiful Baby" Atco

1961 "Irresistible You" Atco

1962 "What'd I Say (Part 1)" Atco

1962 "Things" Atco

1962 "If A Man Answers/All By Myself" Capitol

1962 "Baby Face" Atco

1962 "I Found a New Baby" Atco

1963 "You're the Reason I'm Living" Capitol

1963 "18 Yellow Roses" Capitol

1963 "Treat My Baby Good" Capitol

1963 "Be Mad Little Girl" Capitol

1964 "I Wonder Who's Kissing Her Now" Capitol

1964 "Milord" Atco

1964 "Swing Low Sweet Chariot" Atco

1964 "The Things In This House" Capitol

1965 "Minnie The Moocher" Atco

1965 "Hello, Dolly!" Capitol

1965 "Venice Blue (Que C'est Triste Venise)" Capitol

1965 "When I Get Home" Capitol

1965 "Gyp The Cat" Capitol

1966 "We Didn't Ask To Be Brought Here" Atlantic

1966 "Silver Dollar" Atlantic

1966 "Mame" Atlantic

1966 "Who's Afraid Of Virginia Woolf?" Atlantic

1966 "If I Were a Carpenter" Atlantic

1966 "The Girl That Stood Beside Me" Atlantic

1966 "Lovin' You" Atlantic

1966 "The Lady Came From Baltimore" Atlantic

1967 "Darling Be Home Soon" Atlantic

1967 "Talk to the Animals" Atlantic

1968 "Long Line Rider" Direction

1969 "Me & Mr. Hohner" Direction

1969 "Distractions (Part 1)" Direction

1970 "Sugar Man (9 to 5)" Direction

1970 "Baby May" Direction

1970 "Maybe We Can Get It Together" Direction

1971 "Melody" Motown

1971 "Simple Song of Freedom" Motown

1972 "Sail Away" Motown

1973 "Average People" Motown

1973 "Happy" Motown

1979 "Dream Lover" UK Lightning

1987 "Beyond the Sea" Atlantic

FILMS

Pepe (1960)

Come September (1961)

Too Late Blues (1962)

State Fair (1962)

Hell Is for Heroes (1962)

If a Man Answers (1962)

Pressure Point (1962)

Captain Newman, M.D. (1963)

That Funny Feeling (1965)

Gunfight in Abilene (1967)

Stranger in the House (1967)

Cop Out (1968)

The Happy Ending (1969)

Run, Stranger, Run (1973)